CW00868034

Only
Save Your Kids

Teen Drug Use and How to Stop It

Michael J. Reznicek, M.D.

DEDICATION

To families who have been affected by substance abuse
and who are looking for answers.

CONTENTS

ACKNOWLEDGMENTS

To my wife, Linda, who has contributed to the philosophical development of the following ideas, and who has edited this and many other manuscripts; and to the friends and family members with whom I've been privileged to debate human nature—both its beauty and sordidness.

i

1 BACKGROUND

I cannot think of any need in childhood as strong as the need for a father's protection.

Sigmund Freud

The most recent surveys on teen drug use show that almost half of high school seniors have used illicit drugs. While this figure has remained stable for several years, today's drugs are cheaper and more habit-forming than those of previous generations. The use of crystal methamphetamine, for example, often turns into a habit after just a few uses and a mere $20 can keep a teenager high all weekend.

Most habits start early in life. Childhood is the time to develop habits that lead to success later: a strong work ethic, emotional fortitude, a passion for education, and good social skills. When children enter the drug subculture, they develop habits that lead to failure later in life: slothfulness, disrespect, lawlessness, deception, and anarchy. Children must be protected from these at all costs.

I've been a psychiatrist for over 20 years. I've treated children and adults in a variety of settings. I have experienced substance abuse in close family members and was once a substance abuser myself. No aspect of this problem is foreign to me.

My experience has taught me that keeping teens drug-free doesn't require psychiatrists, medical doctors, therapists or counselors. Not only does it not require them, in most cases you should probably avoid them. The professionals within the substance abuse industry have an agenda to push, and it's helping them a lot more than it's helping people who have drug habits.

The disease model of substance abuse

The biggest mistake we've made in the war against drugs has been to medicalize the problem. Check any government website on drug abuse, or talk to any medical provider, and you'll be told that drug abuse is a brain disease and that treatment is necessary to stop the behavior.[i]

This is nonsense. The disease model grew out of the progressive political tradition of the early 20th century when politicians wanted scientific solutions to social problems. Drug and alcohol abuse, which traditionally had been viewed as a character issue, was redefined as a brain disease. This revolutionary change produced the drug rehab industry and the common belief that this was a job for professionals.

The problem is that this new approach never arose from scientific research. It was developed by a group of individuals who were sensitive to the prevailing political winds. They were the early members of Alcoholics Anonymous and they promoted the disease theory to boost their membership. The scientific community eventually got on board, but only after federal and state governments pushed the issue. The science was shaped to get the funding.

At first glance the science can look compelling. Everyone has seen the colorful images of brain scans showing the effects of drugs on the brain. The images typically depict the biological correlates of craving and withdrawal symptoms that increase the urge to use drugs. Disease experts claim that these urges cause loss-of-control and force users into a state of compulsive use.

Here's where an over-reliance on scientific models misses the bigger picture. Whether people satisfy their urges depends in large part on what they expect to be the consequences of their actions. This is as true for the cocaine addict as it is for the toddler—there exist consequences that, when compelling enough, will redirect the behavior of each. This accounts for the widespread observation that substance abusers don't change until they "hit bottom", the point where the consequences of drug use finally outweigh its benefits. When people quit, their brains naturally return to their normal states, and craving and withdrawal symptoms go away.

When parents learn that they have a substance-abusing child, the most important intervention is to block all access to drugs and to their drug-using friends. I don't recommend drug rehab, as I'll explain below, and mental health counseling is rarely necessary. In the midst of the turmoil that usually accompanies a child being caught, taking complete control of your child's life is all that is needed.

Parents often hear that kids use drugs to self-medicate depression, low self-esteem or other mental problems. The simple truth is that in almost all cases, kids use drugs to appear "cool", rebellious and to become part of an edgy, thrill-seeking social group.

Since all adolescents struggle with moodiness and low self-esteem, these can't be used as explanations for drug use. All adolescents also have a strong need to belong to a social group. If your kids are part of a drug-using group, the answer is to forcibly take them out of it, and steer them into a non-drug group. Forcing a child into counseling might make him think he has a mental defect; it might also make him think that you think he has a mental defect.

The problem with drug rehab

Drug rehab is not really treatment, as much as indoctrination into the disease model. This is the last thing you want your children to learn. In rehab they'll hear that substance abuse is a brain disease and that they have a genetic defect. They'll begin to see themselves as victims and learn that relapses are part of the illness. The disease model also provides redemption for all the wild, destructive things done under the influence—everything is now seen as a symptom of the disease. The take-home message for kids: "You're not responsible for your behavior."

Rehab also connects kids to other drug users. You might imagine that they sit around talking about how they're trying to kick the habit. More likely, they're boasting about their drug use and sharing tips on how they deceived their parents.

If you listen to the experts, they'll say that treatment is necessary to stop drug use. This is simply not true. Most people quit habit-forming drugs with no help at all. And don't expect rehab to get kids motivated to give up drugs. Experts at the prestigious Institute of Medicine say that appeals to motivation are inconsistent with the disease model. [ii] In fact, they're right. If substance abuse is a disease, then there's no basis to expect children to exert the willpower or make the decision to stay drug-free. This is why patients in rehab are rarely admonished to stay sober; instead they're admonished to stay in treatment.

Rehab creates a lot of drama around drug use. When kids are using, they're viewed as victims. When sober, they're "in recovery", a precarious state anchored to the low expectations of the disease model. Parents, too, have been dumbed-down. They often feel helpless, but console themselves by driving kids to rehab appointments. "I'm not a doctor" is a sad but oft-heard expression from parents.

What really works?

Real help is much closer to home. Drug abuse is not a disease, it's a habit. Habits are practiced as long as they bring comfort and are abandoned when they cause pain. And all habits make changes to the brain. Whether one spends time smoking cocaine or practicing the piano, the brain undergoes predictable changes based on the demands placed on it. This is known as neuroplasticity. Quit placing those demands and the changes go away.

The key to keeping children drug-free is to completely block their involvement with drugs and with the drug subculture. This requires parents and extended family members who are tough-minded and willing to practice tough-love. Parents have to make drug use so uncomfortable that it becomes painful, and make sobriety so attractive that it becomes compelling. As comforting as it might be to believe otherwise, the medical profession is not equipped for this task.

The parenting practices discussed in the rest of this book will help all teenagers—those who have never used drugs, and those who currently have drug habits.

2 HERE'S HOW

Most children are not drawn to drugs. They are drawn to pleasing their parents and others in authority. Tell these children to avoid drugs and they'll follow your advice. Other children are naturally self-protective and will figure it out on their own. Not all children, though, are so easily directed. Some are risk-takers. They tend to be restless, show little remorse, and are attracted to the "forbidden fruit". The more you talk about the dangers of drugs, the more they want to try them.

Regardless of the kind of children you have, they'll all benefit from a no-nonsense style of parenting that is clear about expectations and just as clear about consequences. I encourage parents to create written contracts with their children starting in middle school. These contracts should spell out behaviors that are expected and behaviors that are prohibited. The contracts should also list the rewards or punishments for each. Contracts should be modified regularly because incentives change as children age.

Typical punishments for teen substance use might include 3 to 6 months of being grounded, 40 hours of community service, no social use of the car, and cell phones that only call home. If these consequences are explicitly stated ahead of time—and consistently delivered—many children will get the message and steer clear. But the most risk-laden teens will not be deterred. For them, the greater the punishments, the higher the risks, which means they'll be enticed to use even more deception to evade getting caught.

It's especially for these children that I recommend the highly effective intervention of home-based urine drug-testing. Not only does testing break through deception, but non-drug using children are never offended, especially if they know to expect it. Interestingly, government healthcare agencies do not support home drug-testing and the medical profession is strongly opposed to it.

The idea that parents can or should drug-test their children comes as a shock to many, which nicely illustrates the influence of the disease model. Society seems to have decided long ago that responsibility for keeping kids off drugs was a job for the "experts". Parents seeking this control have had to overcome several roadblocks.

In 1996, FDA officials tried to block the sale of home-based drug kits by claiming that they were too complicated for parents. They also felt parents wouldn't know how to handle positive tests. Congress over-rode this FDA arrogance and now these tests are widely available on the internet for as little as $2 (for a single-drug panel) to $7 (for a 5-drug panel). And they are no more difficult to conduct and interpret than a home pregnancy test.

The American Academy of Pediatrics came out against home-based testing in a 2004 article[iii] over concerns that testing might decrease "honest communication between parents and teens." The article also expressed concerns about "whether parents could ever obtain free, informed consent for drug testing from their own child." The Academy recommended that a "professional trained in the interpretation of drug tests" supervise all drug-testing.

The problem with this opposition—other than the obvious professional self-interest—is that no pediatric professional or testing expert is going to be available at 1 a.m.

when your daughter breaks curfew and is acting strange. You need to test her then, and not a week later when you finally get an appointment. The communication concern is also a red herring: if parents tell their children in advance that they'll be tested, the only issue of honesty is whether the parents are going to keep their word. If a test is negative (no evidence of drugs), then parents will have more reason to trust their child; if the test is positive, it can only open the door to more honest communication.

The Office of National Drug Control Policy runs a program called the National Youth Anti-Drug Media Campaign (see www.theantidrug.com). While the website contains useful information for parents, it steers clear of recommending home drug-testing. Instead, it recommends taking your child to a healthcare professional. But if pediatricians are concerned about gaining informed consent from your child, you're not likely to leave the clinic any wiser.

The behavioral contracts discussed above should spell out: 1) that drug use will not be allowed, 2) that children will be randomly drug-tested until they leave home, 3) that parents reserve the right to test whenever they are suspicious, and 4) what the consequences will be for a failed drug test. Parents can modify the contracts to suit their needs. For instance, they could offer rewards for clean drug tests. They need to specify too that any refusal to submit a test will be handled like a positive drug test.

Home drug-testing is best done as part of a comprehensive plan of protection. Parents should get to know the parents of their teens' friends. They should ensure that social activities have adult supervision and parents should prohibit their children from socializing with known drug-users. Parents should always provide structured supervised activities: sports, music lessons, volunteer work, employment, chores at home, tutoring sessions, etc. Keeping children productive is very important for success. Families should also have their own traditions and customs that give children a sense of belonging. Regular sit-down family meals, a shared religious faith, connectedness with the extended family and meaningful traditions around holidays always give children a sense of belonging and significance.

Home drug-testing gives teens a compelling excuse to resist peer pressure: "No thanks, my parents test me." More importantly, testing keeps children honest. Drug-using teens are notoriously dishonest and go to great lengths to deceive their parents. They often develop double-lives: superficial compliance at home and school while they sink deeper into the drug underworld. Testing is the only technique that breaks through this deceit. When teens throw the trust issue in their parents' faces, parents should remind children that trust is always earned.

Teens respect parents who take this no-nonsense approach, especially if they know ahead of time what to expect. I know one young lady who can't wait to be tested again because she knows her clean test will earn her a new outfit.

Parents hold the keys to keeping kids drug-free. They should not be seduced into thinking that the task is too technical or would be better left to the "experts".

I'll present two stories of adolescent drug use; one that is managed poorly, and the other, properly. These are composites of the many cases I have seen from my work in child and adolescent clinics, from talking to family members and friends, and from listening to the stories of the prisoners I treat, almost all of whom were substance abusers as teens.

3 HARD-CORE CORY

There was nothing in Cory's early childhood that would have predicted the path he took. He was an adorable toddler and was part of a large, close-knit, extended family. He loved being the center of attention, which was not unusual for a first-born. He was also sensitive; he cried whenever he was scolded.

Cory was fearless and a risk-taker. He chased balls into the street without checking for traffic. He climbed higher than other children, and he was always drawn to the company of older boys, especially those given to pranks and anything that looked devious.

Cory's parents divorced in grade school and his father started another family in a distant town. Beginning in the seventh grade, when boys enter that awkward stage of growth spurts and self-doubt, Cory found solace by hanging out with a group of boys noted for their dark clothing and heavy-metal music. They were cool. They smoked cigarettes. They hated school. They also smoked marijuana.

Marijuana was a badge of defiance but it also provided a tranquil, agreeable high. Cory and his friends would smoke prior to the start of the school day. They would derisively laugh at the straight kids. They mocked their teachers along with the slogans from DARE classes. Junior high became a smug haze.

Cory talked his mom into allowing him to spend most Friday and Saturday nights at friends' homes. When she questioned his plans, or sought to coordinate with other parents, Cory became angry and accused her of not trusting him. She found it easier to back down.

During these weekends, Cory would check-in periodically and return Sunday evenings. What his mom didn't know was that Cory was spending weekends at young-adult party-houses. Alcohol, LSD, ecstasy, cocaine and marijuana were regular weekend fare. Since drugs cost money, Cory and his friends—being the youngest members of the crowd—were pressed into thievery and burglary. Shoplifting and car prowling provided the necessary fodder for pawn-shop funded weekends. Cory also pressured his mom into buying expensive coats, shoes and jeans, which he then returned for cash. When his mom wondered what happened to the missing items, Cory fabricated stories about thieves. Sometimes she repurchased the items only to see them disappear again.

Cory's grades dropped and he became more hostile at home. In the 9th grade Cory got caught shoplifting. Juvenile probation ordered drug counseling. By the tenth grade, truancy grew in step with a new methamphetamine habit, which provided such a physiological jolt that Cory, on the occasion of his first meth high, resolved that there was no greater experience in life.

Cory soon learned how easy it was to monitor movements in the neighborhood and break into homes when people were away. At age 16, he was caught and spent 30 days in juvenile detention. His parents hired an influential attorney who got the charges dropped on the condition that Cory attend drug rehab and complete one year of supervision. He learned to carry a vial of clean urine on him at all times. He was drug-tested twice that year and passed both times. He graduated from rehab with flying colors. He knew what they wanted to hear.

He came to realize that thievery and burglary were too risky. Selling drugs was safer because both parties wanted a quiet, conflict-free transaction. Selling was also far more lucrative. Cory could support his drug habit and clear about $500 dollars each week with no more than one delivery per day. He learned from his mentors the economic value of a more aggressive approach to debt collection. He started to rough up those who were late with payments. His peers feared him. He wore expensive clothes and jewelry. He was able to buy gifts for his mom, who in turn placed fewer demands on him.

His drug habit grew worse. He lost weight and became paranoid. He started to think everyone was watching him. At the age of 17 he became acutely psychotic after a several-day meth binge. He was taken to the local psychiatric hospital where he fought imaginary demons.

Upon discharge he went to a 45-day inpatient adolescent rehab program in a rural ranch setting. His mother's insurance only paid half the cost of the $34,000 price tag. She took out a second mortgage for the other half. Cory actually enjoyed this inpatient experience. He knew his life was out-of-control. He ate and slept well, gained weight, played basketball during recreation therapy, and took part in many other structured activities. He had meaningful moments with his mother during family counseling.

Cory and his peers did well in this program and not because they were being deceptive. They were teens, after all, so their optimism and invincibility were natural. The adults around them mistook this posture for an embrace of the sober lifestyle. More accurately, these were risk-laden, experience-heavy drug addicts who were frolicking like kids. Rehab had become one more pleasurable experience. The tempo was upbeat, the catharsis was refreshing, and the boys and girls in the program quickly befriended each other. It was widely known, albeit unspoken, that Cory and his friends wouldn't be sober for long.

Shortly after discharge Cory resumed his drug habit. He didn't fall back into it as much as he embraced it. It was what he knew. It was where he had power and influence. Sure, he had some ambivalence, but he knew he had safety net. He was coasting smoothly when tragedy happened. During a contentious drug transaction, eighteen year-old Cory became extremely paranoid and pulled out a gun and killed one of his customers.

Cory's family was devastated. They pooled resources to pay for a private lawyer. He still received a 15-year sentence.

Today Cory sits in the state prison. At the age of 23 he is sober, physically fit, sane, and has a job making uniforms. He's learning to play the guitar. He attends chapel services every week. He has spent two 40-day periods in solitary confinement after fighting off inmates who were pressuring him to join gangs. They leave him alone now, as most people do. His parents occasionally visit. His grandparents send Christmas and birthday cards. Naturally, he regrets the path he took. He blames no one but himself. He says that drug treatment was a joke. "Rehab doesn't make you quit. No one quits until they're ready. You have to want it. I didn't want it until it was too late."

4 MOODY MONICA

Monica was a shy, quiet young girl who did well in school, but spent a lot of time in her room. She lived with an emotionally-labile mother and a father who was distant and stern. Her parents fought often, and they seemed to be more concerned with the needs of her two, much younger siblings.

The family moved across town just prior to the start of high school. Monica felt isolated and inadequate. She had no friends and none of the other students seemed to like her. Eventually, a group of kids approached her. They were vibrant, outgoing, edgy, and cool. They brought marijuana and ecstasy to school. After becoming part of the group, Monica decided to take the risks and try the drugs. They opened up a whole new Monica. Her friends liked her and she got in touch with a wild, new part of herself. She began to tune out her parents.

It was her antagonistic behavior and falling grades that first raised red flags. After her parents found marijuana in her dresser, they followed the recommendation of the school counselor and took her to an adolescent rehab clinic. The experts concluded that she had a "co-occurring disorder". Monica was said to have a chemical dependency problem and a clinical depression that was related to the move. Towards the end of 9th grade, she attended a 30-day treatment program, got on an antidepressant, and seemed to be doing better.

After returning to school in the fall, she quit taking her antidepressant, refused to go to counseling, defied her parents and wholeheartedly adopted the goth dress-code of her peers. She denied that she was using drugs. The school recommended taking her back to the mental health clinic, which they did, but Monica was unruly and defiant. The psychologist recommended that they consider another evaluation at the rehab center.

Monica's parents were looking for other ideas. Their daughter was at a crucial point in her development. At 16 years of age, she was headed for disaster. The family had large out-of-pocket expenses for both rehab and therapy, and after the last round, they couldn't afford any more. They were also skeptical of her treatment. They knew the kind of girl she had been. Underneath the crust of defiance and lies, there was a confused, but sweet young lady. They knew how much her new peer group influenced her. They began to believe that Monica's problems stemmed not from a brain disease, but from being a typical adolescent. She had feelings of inadequacy and wanted to be accepted by her peers.

Monica's parents took action once they realized that an adolescent's feelings should never be allowed to run the show. They followed my advice to go to the drug store and buy over-the-counter drug testing panels. They were to hold Monica at home until she submitted a specimen. I had warned them that Monica likely would put off the testing long enough to consume large amounts of water in the hope of diluting her urine. Just as predicted, she didn't void for hours, but when she did, she tested positive for marijuana and cocaine.

It wasn't just Monica who had to change. Her parents realized that they too had to make adjustments. Their daughter had gotten into trouble in part because they had not been paying attention. They felt guilty. But they soon realized that Monica had a mind of her own. Even if they had done everything correctly, she still might have taken this path. Parents can't take responsibility for everything a child does, but they can take responsibility for everything they do.

Monica's parents decided to redo the structure and routines of the family. They wanted to protect Monica, of course, but they also wanted to prevent this from happening to her younger brothers. They developed a comprehensive plan that completely insulated Monica from her drug-using friends. They withdrew her from school and enrolled her in a private religious school. They completely blocked all connections to her former peer group. They took away her cell phone, car keys and restricted access to the internet. She was confined to home except for supervised school activities. She spent weekends with her parents working on home improvement projects, church functions or community service activities. Her parents supervised homework during the evenings. She made friends at her new school, but with the non-drug users. Monica didn't have enough unsupervised free-time to run with the druggies. She didn't go out on Friday and Saturday nights except for outings that her parents or other adults supervised. For two summers during high school she worked on her grandparents' farm.

Monica's parents gradually released her restrictions. She got a job during the school year and they allowed her to have a boyfriend. They randomly drug-tested Monica until she became an adult. She never again visited a rehab clinic. She also never tested positive again. Today, Monica thinks her parents might have gone too far, but she admits they did what they did because they love her. She also notes that her parents seem happier as a couple.

5 WRITING BEHAVIORAL CONTRACTS

There is no better way to structure a child's life than with a coherent, written plan in the form of a behavioral contract. These should include the following elements: 1) a list of behaviors to encourage, 2) a list of behaviors to discourage or prohibit, and 3) specific rewards or punishments for each. Parents must consistently monitor their child's behavior and carry out the terms of the contract. They also need to rewrite contracts at regular intervals because incentives change as children age.

Contracts that deal with drug use and other adult behaviors should be written no later than the start of middle school. This is the time when children are commonly exposed to such behaviors, and the time when many children start going astray. Contracts should be posted in a private part of the home that is not observable by guests who don't have a need-to-know.

While it's best to have contracts that are mutually agreed upon, this isn't always possible. Not all children will cooperate. If this is the case, parents should still write a contract and post it. Parents are the legal and moral authorities in their families, and their rules and expectations are not subject to a child's veto anyway. But if a child participates and feels like he has been part of the process, then he'll have more ownership in the authority of the contract and a harder time disputing it.

Single parents, especially moms, often have difficulty with risk-laden teenage sons. It's best to have strong adult males—uncles, grandfathers, pastors—present to validate and enforce written contracts. Most teenage boys respect only one thing: power. If you bring powerful men into a young boy's life, he'll be much easier to control and he'll develop the requisite humility to succeed in life.

Children want to know the rules and expectations that apply to them. They also want to be protected. The reason many kids join gangs is that the rules are clear, disobedience is not tolerated, and they get the protection they crave. Children are drawn to this kind of power and clarity. Parents and teachers should take a few cues from gang leaders.

Contracts deflect many family conflicts. Parents are able to maintain more composure because they can redirect hostility onto that piece of paper—the contract. When children violate the contract, parents can say, "Oh, Jason, I'm so sorry. I was hoping that we wouldn't have to deliver this consequence but that contract forces my hand." Jason's anger can then be directed at the contract.

Tips on developing target behaviors

Behaviors should generally be listed in positive, desirable language. For instance, "Grades will be C's, B's and A's", is better than "No D's or F's" Another example: "Always be kind to your sisters" is better than "Do not be mean to your sisters". The negative formulation in this case leaves open the option of just ignoring his sisters, which is not kind. Better to be positive and kind, since those are the attributes that parents want to instill.

The technological revolution has made parental monitoring more efficient and accurate. For instance, schools now have portals where parents can logon and see a child's day-to-day progress and current grades. Parents can also install GPS monitoring software (www.vehicle-tracking-gps.com) in their cars to track where their children have gone and how fast they travelled to get there. You can even have the system text you if certain parameters have been exceeded. Computer monitoring software exists (www.spectorsoft.com) to track which websites your kids have visited, the content of their emails and text messages if delivered on the computer. And all cell phone calls are listed on your monthly bill, which can be viewed at any time on your wireless carrier's website.

Sample positive behaviors:

- Make your bed and straighten your bedroom every morning before school.
- You are allowed to take the car only to places where you have permission to go.
- Drug tests are always clean.
- All school assignments will be turned in on time.
- Always shows respect for Mom and Dad.
- Always performs scheduled chores.
- Always set an example for your younger brothers and sisters to follow.
- Always owns responsibility for personal behavior.

Tips on developing consequences and rewards

Rewards and punishments must be relevant and powerful enough to motivate. I don't recommend that rewards be too lavish. Obeying the rules, after all, should be an expected norm. Consequences should be sufficiently severe to act as deterrents ("Grounded for 30 days") without crushing the spirit of your child ("Grounded until you turn 18"). Not all consequences should be construed as punitive; many might better be viewed as character-building, such as "20 hours of volunteer work at the animal shelter".

Punishments tend to work best if they reflect something a parent can control, rather than compelling a child to act. For instance, "No cell phone for a week" might be a preferred punishment over "Clean the living room every day for a week". The latter can set up a 7-day battle over trying to get your child in the cleaning mood. Parents should ensure that they're not working harder than their teens in fulfilling the obligations of the contracts.

Another example: if you want to check your children's homework, make sure they're responsible for bringing it to you, rather than you having to ask for it. The contracts can list suitable consequences if children don't present their homework.

Remember that the most potent punishments for teenagers will be whatever takes away their freedoms or connections to their peers: the car, the cell phone, the internet and being allowed to go out on weekends. It won't take too many times of losing these privileges before you see marked improvements in their behavior.

Conclusion

A child's world is filled with positive and negative incentives. A parent's task is to be creative enough to see them. When parents do, they'll be able to move their children in the direction they want them to go.

Effective parenting often takes the form of President Teddy Roosevelt's maxim: "Speak softly and carry a big stick." Clear rules and tough consequences will maintain order in any home. Yelling or other displays of wild emotions are neither necessary nor helpful.

This is the value of behavioral contracts. They prevent confusion, enabling and over-reacting. They also avoid the inconsistencies of trying to establish rules on the fly. Teenagers have little emotional control and they'll look for cracks to exploit. Expect wild reactions from them, but don't retaliate in kind. Planning ahead, when things are calm, can prevent a lot of mistakes.

Delivering consequences for childhood misbehavior can be done with few if any comments. Let the "big stick" of pre-announced consequences do most of the talking.

Sample abbreviated contract

Target behavior	Time-frame	Reward	Consequence
Is always kind to your sisters.	Every 2 weeks	One extra Netflix rental for the weekend.	No video games for 24 hours for each infraction.
Grades are C and above	Each semester	$10 per A, $7 per B, $3 per C.	No sleepovers until grades are C or above.
Clean drug test	Each episode	None. This is expected behavior.	Grounded for 60 days. No cell phone use, no car and no internet except for homework. Volunteer 40 hrs of reading time at the nursing home.
Completes all scheduled chores without being asked.	Each week	Usual liberties on the weekend.	Grounded for the weekend.

6 HOW TO HOME DRUG-TEST

If parents choose to drug-test their children, it's best to let them know this ahead of time. For most kids it will act as a deterrent. Parents should specify that they reserve the right to drug-test any time they want and that any refusal to submit a specimen will be treated like a positive test. While testing is important, it's not necessary to do battle with your child. If they refuse to cooperate, simply treat it as a failed drug test—as if they've been using drugs. This is how it's done in the adult workplace. Home drug-testing gets kids ready for the real world.

Here's another dynamic you can weave into the testing: parents can offer a "reduced sentence" if a child confesses to drug use prior to the testing. If a child thinks the test will find him guilty, he'll have an incentive to confess. If so, this would solve the problem of the occasional false-negative (the child has been using drugs, but the level in the urine is low enough that it doesn't register.) Offers like this are common in the criminal justice system; they're called plea bargains.

Sophisticated drug-using teens often use elaborate means to escape detection. Some will keep in their possession a vial of "clean" urine from a non-drug using friend. Others will store a vial of clean urine in the bathroom—under the sink or in the ducts. If parents don't want to directly observe a child urinating into a specimen cup, then ensure that no clean urine is accessible. Don't let your child carry any items into the bathroom except the specimen cup you provide. When returned, the specimen should be warm and yellow. If it's cold or room temperature, it's not their urine. If it's colorless, they may have anticipated the test and drank a lot of fluid to dilute their urine with the hope of coming in under the threshold. It's possible, too, that they filled the cup with tap water.

Many people—adults and children—have difficulty urinating under pressure. It's called "shy bladder". If this happens, reassure your child that this is a common problem. The solution is to relax as much as possible and wait. Have your child do homework or read while you wait with him. Don't let your child go to a friend's house. The bladder will need to empty eventually. Drinking sips of water can help.

When testing the urine, be sure to follow the instructions that come with your tests. Give your child a disposable testing cup and have them fill it half-way. Remove the test card from the sealed pouch. Pull the cap from the end of the test card, and dip the strips into the urine to the level indicated. Immerse the tips for 10 to 15 seconds, or whatever is recommended. Replace the cap and place the card on a non-absorbent flat surface. Generally the results are read at about 5 minutes. All control lines should appear. If there has been no drug use, all the test lines should also appear. If a test line does not appear, then it should be considered evidence that your child has been using that drug.

Be aware that some prescription medications can be detected on urine drug tests. If your child has been prescribed codeine for cough suppression, it can show up positive for "opiates". Sudafed and other cold preps containing pseudoephedrine can cause positive results for "amphetamines". But don't be taken in by claims that second-hand smoke was responsible for a positive marijuana test. The amount of second-hand smoke exposure that is required to turn the test positive is so great that your child should face consequences for spending so much time around pot smokers. The test doesn't turn positive by walking past someone who is smoking.

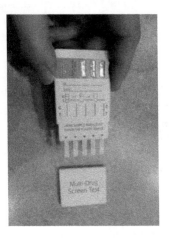

This 5-way test detects cocaine, marijuana, opiates, amphetamine and methamphetamine, and sells for less than $5.

A saliva test for alcohol

Home alcohol tests are also available and are highly sensitive (see picture next page). Have your child spit onto the end of the test strip. At 2 minutes, compare it to the scale on the back of the package. Any color change indicates that your child has been drinking. A box of 24 of these costs under $40. See at www.alco-screen.com.

Some children will try to sabotage alcohol tests by rinsing with Listerine when they get home. This will also produce a positive result and they'll use it to deflect the fact that they were out drinking. If you plan to test for alcohol, do it as soon as children walk through the door. Remember, don't argue or fight over this test. If your child fails to fully cooperate, treat it like a positive test. And tell them they're not allowed to use mouthwash when they come home.

This simple saliva test for alcohol is available on the internet for under $2.

Where to buy home drug-tests

Home drug-tests can be purchased at local pharmacies or online. You'll pay more for tests at the drugstore, but they have the added convenience of being available the night you need them. If you plan ahead, you can order single-drug tests, such as for marijuana or alcohol, for under $2. Multiple-drug panels are available for more, but usually don't exceed $5 to $7 each.

There is great price variability on the internet, but real bargains can be found like those listed above. Check out the following sites:

www.drugalcoholtest.com
www.homehealthtesting.com
www.testcountry.com
www.testmyteen.com

7 SIGNS OF DRUG USE

Keeping kids drug-free would be easier if there were clear and unmistakable signs. Unfortunately, this is not usually the case. Sure, you might be able to smell alcohol on your child's breath, or detect marijuana smoke on her clothing, but drug-using children are pretty good at hiding what they do and many drugs don't leave traces. Some kids will also make a concerted effort to be more respectful and helpful at home for the very reason that they don't want to set off warning bells.

Detection is also complicated by the fact that the signs of drug use are often the same signs of normal adolescence: moodiness, irritability, arguing, slacking, anger, appetite changes, withdrawal from family, bad grades, and excessive sleeping. Parents have to make sure they don't assume that such behavior is indicative of drug use, or that happy, compliant behavior is a sign of no drug use.

What follows is a list of drugs of abuse and several signs that all parents should know.

Marijuana

The smell of marijuana is easily detected by those who are familiar with it. It has a sweet, musty aroma and can usually be detected on clothing. Marijuana can also cause bloodshot eyes and the "munchies". Excessive and inappropriate laughter is also common.

Sedative-hypnotics

These drugs include barbiturates (phenobarbital, Seconal) and benzodiazepines (Valium, Ativan, Klonopin, Xanax). These drugs mimic the signs of alcohol: unsteady gait, clumsiness, slurred speech and inappropriate comments.

Cocaine

This drug can be snorted, smoked or injected. Cocaine powder is snorted, usually through tightly-wound dollar bills or straws. Crack cocaine, which is more highly concentrated, is smoked. Cocaine usually makes the user feel euphoric and energetic, and leads to increases in body temperature, blood pressure, and heart rate. Seizures, abdominal pain, and nausea can result. The appetite is usually suppressed; regular users often lose weight. This has been a common weight-loss agent over the years, especially for women.

Methamphetamine

This is a very habit-forming stimulant that is a concentrated form of amphetamine. It causes intense, energetic highs that increase the heart rate and blood pressure. It's a white, odorless, bitter-tasting powder that is snorted or injected. It has a rock-like version called "crystal meth" that is heated and smoked. Like cocaine, this will also cause extreme weight loss and insomnia. Users can stay up for days on end and then sleep for days when they come off the drug. Meth use can also lead to profound behavioral changes that include paranoia, restlessness ("tweaking") and abrupt acts of violence.

Ecstasy (MDMA)

This is a tablet or capsule that causes feelings of mental stimulation, emotional warmth, enhanced sensory perception, and increased energy. Adverse health effects can include nausea, chills, sweating, teeth clenching, muscle cramping, and blurred vision. MDMA can interfere with the body's ability to regulate temperature, which can occasionally be fatal if the body overheats. This drug is commonly used at "rave" parties and at nightclubs.

LSD (acid)

LSD produces unpredictable psychological "trips" that produce delusions and hallucinations and last about 12 hours. The effects can be frightening and often lead to panic attacks. Physical effects include increased body temperature, heart rate, and blood pressure. Insomnia and loss of appetite are common. LSD is sold as tablets, capsules, liquid, or on absorbent small squares of paper called "stamps".

Heroin

Heroin is a strong morphine-based drug that is usually injected, though it can be snorted or smoked. Intravenous heroin addicts are called "junkies". Heroin is a strong narcotic pain reliever. Short-term effects include euphoria and clouded thinking followed by alternating wakeful and drowsy states. Users typically "crash", which means they lie around for hours in a somnolent state—think of the 19th century opium dens depicted in movies. In overdose, heroin depresses breathing, which is how heroin junkies often die. Users who inject the drug are at risk for infectious diseases such as HIV/AIDS and hepatitis.

PCP (phencyclidine)

PCP is a synthetic drug sold as tablets, capsules, or as a powder. It can be snorted, smoked, or eaten. It was developed in the 1950s as an anesthetic. Like ketamine discussed below, PCP causes "dissociation"—it distorts perceptions of sight and sound and produces feelings of detachment from the environment and self. At high doses it can cause unpredictable and violent behavior.

Club drugs

These are drugs commonly found in the nightclub scene. They include Ecstasy, methamphetamine, LSD, GHB, Rohypnol®, and ketamine. The first 3 are covered above. GHB and Rohypnol are brain depressants like the sedative-hypnotics. GHB was approved by the Food and Drug Administration in 2002 for use in the treatment of narcolepsy (a sleep disorder). GHB is usually ingested orally, either in liquid or powdered form. Rohypnol (flunitrazepam) is a benzodiazepine like Valium. It has gained popularity in the United States since the early 1990s. Both of these drugs have a reputation as "date rape" drugs. They are odorless, colorless and tasteless. They are usually sold in pill-form and are frequently combined with alcohol and other beverages to incapacitate users.

Ketamine is an anesthetic used in veterinary practice. It causes "dissociation" similar to PCP. High doses can cause dreamlike states, hallucinations, delirium and amnesia.

Prescription drug abuse

Teen substance abusers often steal prescription drugs from family members, either for their own use or to sell for cash. Common prescription drugs that are abused or sold include narcotic pain pills (Oxycontin, Vicodin, Dilaudid and Demerol), stimulants (Ritalin, Adderall, and Concerta), and benzodiazepines (Xanax, Valium, Ativan, and Klonopin).

Part of the reason we have seen an increase in teen prescription drug abuse is that doctors have been writing more prescriptions for these drugs. According to the National Institute on Drug Abuse, between 1991 and 2009, prescriptions for stimulants increased from 5 million to nearly 40 million, which is an 8-fold increase. Prescriptions for narcotic analgesics increased from about 45 million to approximately 180 million, which is a 4-fold increase.

Inhalants

Inhalants are a diverse group of substances whose chemical vapors can be inhaled to produce mind-altering effects. A variety of common household products can be abused: spray paint, some glues, gasoline, paint thinner and cleaning fluids. Young children and adolescents are familiar with this practice. If they haven't "huffed" these substances themselves, then they've heard about kids at school doing it.

The effects of inhalants are similar to those of alcohol and include slurred speech, lack of coordination, euphoria, and dizziness. Inhalants can also cause lightheadedness, hallucinations, delusions, confusion, nausea and vomiting.

By displacing air in the lungs, inhalants deprive the body of oxygen, which can damage cells throughout the body, but the cells of the brain are especially sensitive. Permanent memory problems or slowed thinking can result. High concentrations of inhalants can also cause death.

Drug paraphernalia

These are items that are used to help transport or consume drugs. They include pipes, syringes, needles and roach clips. The latter is for holding the burning end of a marijuana cigarette. Paraphernalia also includes razor blades, spoons, tightly-rolled dollar bills, straws, empty pen casings, digital scales, vials, and small Ziploc baggies.

Light bulbs are often used to smoke methamphetamine. The metal cap is removed and meth is heated inside the bulb in order to vaporize it prior to smoking. I've talked to parents who began noticing that light bulbs were missing from their home. This led to the discovery that their son was a meth addict. Other meth paraphernalia includes bottle caps and pieces of foil.

A note about drug-testing

Home drug-tests do not detect all the drugs listed above. There is no test, for instance, that identifies LSD, GHB or inhalants. On the other hand, most teen drug users concurrently use marijuana and alcohol, which are readily detectable. By identifying these, parents will be able to identify most drug-using children.

8 PARENTAL GUILT

Nothing can be as satisfying as raising a child, but nothing is more prone to emotional pain than raising a child.

We all make mistakes in life, whether through miscalculations, carelessness, or getting derailed by our own addictive behavior. Life also forces us to make unwanted decisions, such as divorce or having to work far from home. When circumstances adversely affect children, parents often feel bad and respond in ways that can make matters worse, such as being too permissive or too angry.

When children are caught using drugs, parents often experience anger, guilt, shame or all three. It's important to identify these emotions because parents react to them differently. Ideally, we would first identify our emotions and then plan a response. Instead, we usually react impulsively, and with little thought. Only later do we notice whether or not we responded appropriately. This is not the best way to do things.

Feelings of guilt indicate that we've done something wrong. It usually involves something we could have done differently, such as provided more supervision. Guilt means our children were hurt by our actions. Shame, on the other hand, is a more pernicious emotion. Shame indicates that we are concerned that our child has made us look bad *in the eyes of others*. Shame is a concern about our own image. Guilt is a concern for our children.

Research[iv] has shown that when parents feel shamed by a child's behavior, they tend to react in maladaptive ways, such as yelling, using overly harsh discipline or withdrawing and using inattention as a form of punishment.

Guilt, on the other hand, tends to result in reactions that are more adaptive, such as explaining why a behavior was wrong and how to behave more appropriately in the future.

Thus guilt is much preferred over shame. Dealing with shame is beyond the scope of this book, but it requires serious self-examination and rethinking one's place and purpose in the world. Guilt, though, is very useful and should be used to motivate us. That said, we shouldn't distort guilt and make it something other than a concern for our children. Some tend to exaggerate guilt when they have narcissistic tendencies: "I'm such a good parent; how could I have ever done such a thing?" Some enhance guilt by comparing themselves to others: "They're the ideal family; they never make mistakes."

The antidote to such thinking is to accept the fact that each of us is flawed—and deeply so. We all make mistakes with our children. If it appears that others don't, then we don't know them very well.

We deal with guilt by using it to force us to start doing what is right—today.

The serenity prayer applies here: "God grant me the serenity to accept the things I cannot change; courage to change the things I can; and wisdom to know the difference." The past can't be changed, but the present can.

When parents experience guilt, they should examine the situation and change whatever will prevent it from happening in the future. Careful forethought and planning are key—hence the value of the pre-arranged contracts. Parents can even write down their own "standard operating procedures" to help them be consistent and think clearly when issues arise: "When Rebekah asks to spend the night at a friend's house: 1) check her contract to make sure she is eligible, and 2) discuss it with the other parents before giving permission."

Parents should never lean on their children for emotional support nor should they call attention to their mistakes or shortcomings. Parents can, however, admit their mistakes if children call attention to them, and even when it might appear that parents are hypocrites. In truth, there is nothing hypocritical when you do the right thing for children: "Yes, I did drugs when I was your age, but it was a mistake. I wish people had structured my life like I'm about to do for you."

Kids will sometimes play the guilt-card, but parents should stick to their principles: "It's okay for me to drink alcohol because I'm an adult. I've earned my way in the adult world. You're a child, and haven't yet shown you can do the same. When you're an adult, you can drink alcohol too."

When parents make mistakes, they can partially recover by finding a silver lining in the situation and use it as a teaching moment. "Alexander, I didn't provide the after-school supervision you needed, and you got into trouble. Both of us now have a better understanding of what goes on in this neighborhood when I'm not here."

Parents need to remember that even if they do things right, children have a mind of their own and are capable of defying instruction and making poor choices. When that happens, parents are responsible only for how they respond to those choices, and for evaluating what can be done differently in the future. Especially for older children, there's a limit to how much responsibility parents should absorb.

9 CONCLUSION

The parenting practices that keep children drug-free are the same that produce industrious, honest and mature young men and women. Teens need a lot of supervision and guidance. They're on the threshold of the adult world without the know-how or wisdom to navigate it on their own.

Letting children vegetate in front of the television or giving them substantial unsupervised time with peers creates fertile soil for habits of self-indulgence.

For teens already practicing the drug habit, parents should avoid rehab programs that follow the disease model, which is almost every one of them. The rehab option will sound comforting, but it's expensive, it generates drama and does nothing to compel sobriety. And teens learn plenty of new ways to use drugs while in rehab. In the end, it's important to remember that risk-laden teens respond to consequences, not words.

Another of my incarcerated patients had a cocaine habit that started when he was a teen. He graduated from several rehab programs, which he now says were little more than temporary rescue operations. He said what he needed then was not to be rescued, but to be restrained.

Parents should aggressively restrain their children from street drugs and the drug subculture. Success will come from setting clear expectations, providing close supervision and delivering effective consequences. Parents have to be attentive and smart. Keeping kids drug-free is neither hard to understand nor difficult to manage, as long as one is willing to challenge long-held beliefs about the problem.

What follows is a list of suggested guidelines for setting the tone for responsible behavior around you and your family. It's not an exhaustive list, but it illustrates the principles of effective embedded controls—the kind of attitudes and expectations that create honesty and responsible behavior. Some of these apply not to children but to other adults. These suggestions require no guidance or training from professionals. Most of these controls are instinctive and automatic. They only require that responsible people act in their own self interest and in the interest of their loved ones.

- Show children respect by holding them responsible for their own behavior.
- Never blame drugs or alcohol for irresponsible behavior.
- Be swift to condemn any behavior that adversely affects you or those you love.
- Never apologize for doing so.
- Ostracize irresponsible people from your social circles.
- Protect your financial assets from irresponsible people.
- Call the police if you know that someone is driving under the influence.
- Never make yourself responsible for teaching other adults how to behave.
- Never make yourself responsible for the behavior of other adults.
- Never date a substance abuser.
- Never marry a substance abuser.

- Never provide meals, housing or money to substance abusers.
- Never say to a substance abuser, "you need help".
- Drug counselors are useful only to the extent they can help family members set effective consequences for irresponsible use of drugs or alcohol.
- Substance abusers frequently lie; always be skeptical of them.
- Never try to get the "truth" out of a substance abuser.
- Never bail a substance abuser out of jail.
- Never make excuses for substance abusers.
- Give aid to those who have been adversely affected by substance abusers.
- Get to know the police officers who patrol your neighborhood; they are a wonderful resource when you need someone escorted off your property.
- When former substance abusers appear to have transformed their lives, welcome them back with open arms.
- If they return to the substance abusing habit, send them away.

ABOUT THE AUTHOR

Dr. Michael J. Reznicek is a board-certified psychiatrist with over 20 years of experience. He has practiced in the military, in hospital-based community settings, in prisons, and in state hospitals. He currently practices in the Department of Corrections in Washington state.

Dr. Reznicek has extensive experience in the field of substance abuse. He has written for *The Weekly Standard*, the *Omaha World Herald* and has had letters in the *New York Times*, *Wall Street Journal*, and other publications. He has been a guest on numerous talk-radio shows at the local, national and international levels where he has discussed drug abuse.

He is an outspoken critic of the way psychiatry over-medicalizes human behavior.

He lives in Spokane, Washington with his wife Linda.

ENDNOTES

[i] The National Institute of Drug Abuse claims that treatment is necessary to stop drug abuse. See the NIDA's publication, *"Drugs, Brains and Behavior—The Science of Addictions"*, 2010, National Institutes of Health. See also at: www.nida.nih.gov/scienceofaddiction/treatment.html.

[ii] *Dispelling the Myths About Addiction: Strategies to Increase Understanding and Strengthen Research*, Institute of Medicine, 1997, p. 140. See online at www.nap.edu/catalog.php?record_id=5802

[iii] Levy, S.; Van Hook, S.; and Knight, J.; A Review of Internet-Based Home Drug-Testing Products for Parents, *Pediatrics* 113 (2004), pp. 720-726.

[iv] Scarnier, M., Schmader, T., Lickel, B.; Parental shame and guilt: Distinguishing emotional responses to a child's wrongdoings, *Personal Relationships*, 16 (2009), pp 205-220.

CPSIA information can be obtained
at www.ICGtesting.com
Printed in the USA
BVHW071419090119
537429BV00013B/1225/P